MARRIAGE
MOTIVATOR

The most practical marriage book
THAT EVEN MEN WILL READ.

BRYAN D. ROBERTSON

outskirts
press

Acknowledgements

I would like to thank God for creating marriage and for helping to make it fun and enjoyable. I thank my wife, Kari, for encouraging me and putting up with my A.D.D. and idiosyncrasies. She is a wonderful wife and mother of our four children: Zan, Solomon, Leti, and Lena. She has also been a wonderful mother to eleven foster children. I would also like to thank all of the role models in my family that I have learned from just by watching and observing their marriages. I will have several thoughts and ideas from my family throughout this book.

I have also learned from many pastors who have preached on the topic of marriage. One of the best sermons I've ever heard was from Dr. E. V. Hill when he preached at his wife's funeral. I've listened to that sermon about 25 times. He talks a lot about marriage in that sermon and it has helped so much. You can listen to the audio on YouTube. The title of it is "Baby"—that's what he called his wife. Other pastors and speakers who I've listened to teach on marriage would include but are not limited to: Ross Robertson, Dan Robertson, Dr. Buster Wilson, Jerry East, Dr. Ron Stewart, Andy Stanley, Louie Giglio, Dr. Johnny Hunt, Forrest Sheffield, Dr. Randy Bostick, Dave Ramsey, Dr. Tony Evans, Dave & Ann Wilson, Jeff & Debbie McElroy, Tim Hawkins, Dennis Swanberg, Steve Bennett, Dr. Jim Futral, Dr. Adrian Rogers, Ed Young, Jr., Emmerson Eggerichs, Dr. Gary Chapman, and Dennis Rainey.

Lastly, I would like to thank my accountability partners throughout the years in helping to hold me accountable to the Lord, to purity, to having a consistent quiet time, etc. Accountability has been a ROCK in my development as a born-again believer. These men have sharpened me by asking me the hard questions that most men don't talk about (Proverbs 27:17). See chapter 27 about accountability.

Table of Contents

INTRODUCTION

My wife, Kari, and I met on a blind date. That's right—the dreaded yet exciting "blind date." I had been on one other blind date and it didn't work out too good. Here's how *that* date went: I was in seminary at Mid-America Baptist Theological in Memphis, TN, and interning at Bellevue Baptist Church. Someone recommended that I go out with this girl. I called her and said, "Let's meet at Bellevue and go to church together." So, we met and sat through church, talked a little afterwards, and said "Good-bye." Needless to say, it didn't work out—AWKWARD.

However, with Kari, it was different. My Uncle Dan was her pastor in Pontotoc, Mississippi, and I always asked Uncle Dan if he had found my wife. Pontotoc is only 32 miles from where I grew up in Oxford, MS. Even though that is really nearby, I had never met Kari growing up. Here's a weird thought: when I was a senior in high school, she was a 6th-grader. Anyway, her family had recently joined West Heights Baptist Church where my Uncle Dan was pastoring, and he finally found someone to recommend to me. I was 28 at the time and searching for Mrs. Robertson, and Kari was 22 and the reigning Miss Mississippi, I might add. He called me and told me about Kari and her family. So I called her and tried to tell her about myself and said, "Uncle Dan seems to think we ought to go out on a date." I told her we could go "spit off a bridge or something." Doesn't that sound exciting? Kari said "yes" and so the date was planned. Before our date, Kari was in the Miss America Pageant (Top 10 Finalist) so I had the opportunity to see her on TV before she saw me. Therefore, I was excited about the date!

We went out and had a great time and got married (8-2-1997) within 10 months. Four children and 23 years later, we are going strong and falling more and more in love with each other. Like most marriages, we have had to work on it to make it strong. Just like a muscle, you have to work it to make it strong. Great marriages do not just happen. Haven't you heard of couples that started out so good and they were perfect for each other, but three years later ended up in a divorce? It's not how you start, it's how you grow along the way and ultimately finish that counts.

Chapter 1
BE ENCOURAGED

MOST MARRIAGES MAKE it! There is no need to have a backup plan or to have separate bank accounts. Marriage is one of the greatest things that can happen to you. You are in the strongest commitment and bond in society. You are committed to love and respect, to be faithful and true. You are in it to win it and be successful. You can do this! God is on your side because He created and ordained it. Despite your past, God can make this marriage BEAUTIFUL and a BLESSING. Don't throw in the towel. Don't say the "D" word. Don't even THINK the "D" word. Your marriage is a picture of the Gospel; so let it PREACH! Motivated yet? Keep reading ...

Don't believe the myth that 50 percent of all marriages end in divorce. Here's what Shaunti Feldhahn says in her book *The Good News About Marriage*:

> **The vast majority of marriages last a lifetime; the current divorce rate has never been close to 50 percent—it is closer to 20 to 25 percent for first-time marriages and 31 percent for all marriages—and has been declining for years.**[1]

That's GREAT news! This gives us MORE hope that our marriages will make it! But wait, there's more good news from Feldhahn concerning churchgoers:

> **The rate of divorce in the church is 25 to 50 percent lower than among those who don't attend worship services, and those who prioritize their faith and/or pray together are dramatically happier and more connected.[2]**

This should motivate us to know God more, to love God more, to serve God more, and to worship God more. He will magnify and bless your marriage. God wants you to be an active part of His bride—the church. Don't be just an average attender. Be committed and serve within your giftedness and let the church serve your marriage by attending anything that will strengthen your marriage.

I've held many different roles in churches and we offer marriage classes every fall and spring. We also provide a *Date Night* event and an annual *Marriage Retreat* off campus. We want to enhance and motivate marriages. You want to know why? Here's why: So goes the marriage, so goes the parenting; so goes the parenting, so goes the family; so goes the family, so goes the church; so goes the church, so goes society.

God is for your marriage. Your family and friends are for your marriage (despite what a few naysayers might say). Your children are for your marriage, and the church is here to help your marriage succeed. Hopefully, you attend a church that promotes, supports, and helps marriages. All churches should offer classes, sermon series, seminars, retreats, and the like to help in money matters, parenting, and marriages every year. If we have a healthy balance in these three areas, we can handle the rest of life's issues.

Therefore encourage one another and build each other up, just as in fact you are doing.

1 Thessalonians 5:11

Chapter 2

BE GODLY

MARRIAGE WAS THE creation and invention of God. It is the joining of a man and woman together for life. It is where they make their relationship public, official, and permanent in front of family, friends, and God. Today, ministers perform marriage ceremonies, but God officiated the first marriage in the Garden of Eden between Adam and Eve.

The Bible says in Genesis 2:21–24,

> *So, the LORD God caused a deep sleep to fall upon the man, and he slept; then He took one of his ribs and closed up the flesh at the place. The LORD God fashioned into a woman the rib which He had taken from the man, and brought her to the man. The man said, 'This is now bone of my bones, and flesh of my flesh; she shall be called Woman, because she was taken out of Man.' For this reason, a man shall leave his father and his mother, and be joined to his wife; and they shall become one flesh* (**NASB**).

I'm sure you've heard of the triangle effect in marriage. Here's a diagram of it:

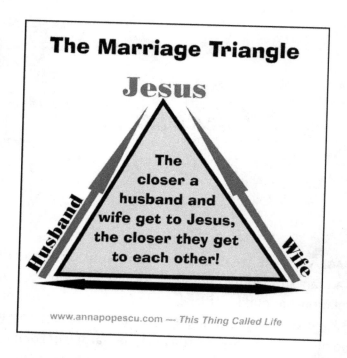

This is so true. God's will for every born-again believer is *"to be conformed into the image of Christ,"* according to Romans 8:29. If this is the husband and wife's focus and purpose, they will definitely grow closer to each other. It's inevitable. The opposite is true as well: the farther away from God they go, the farther apart they will become from each other. Jesus is our bond. In Him is life—*abundant life!* (John 10:10)

So how do you grow closer to God? Here is a list of ways to do so:

- **Worship God**: Sing praises to Him and listen to Christian music. Many people start their devotional time with a song of praise. Music moves you and motivates you. So why not listen to Godly music that will move you in the right direction? Christian music has the power to change a bad day into a great day. Worship helps give you the right perspective on your day. So get your praise on and worship the KING of Kings and LORD of Lords. He is worthy of our worship. Jesus said in Luke 4:8, "*Worship the Lord your God and serve Him only*" (NIV).

- **Talk and listen to God**: This is what it means to pray. It is communication and communion with God. Proverbs 3:6 says, "*in all your ways acknowledge Him, and He shall direct your paths*" (NKJV). We can talk to God about anything and everything. He understands because He made us. Then we must listen. Psalms 46:10(a) reminds us: "*Be still and know that I am God*" (NKJV). In our busy society, it is difficult to be still. We have to be intentional about it. We have to get alone with God and turn the noise off in order to hear His still, small voice.

Oswald Chambers says in his devotional, *My Utmost for His Highest*:

> **We show how little love we have for God by preferring to listen to His servants rather than to Him. We like to listen to personal testimonies, but we don't want God Himself to speak to us. Why are we so terrified for God to speak to us? It is because we know that when God speaks we must either do what He asks or tell Him we will not obey. But if it is simply one of God's servants speaking to us, we feel obedience is optional, not imperative. We respond by saying, 'Well, that's only your own idea, even though I don't deny that what you said is probably God's truth.'[3]**

- **Read God's Word**: Get into the Word of God and let the God of the Word get into you. We should have a quiet time to learn more about God, not to check it off the list. Yes, the will of God is in the Word of God. And yes, the Word of God can help keep you from sin. But the main reason to read the Bible is to get more and more acquainted with God. *"In the beginning was the Word, and the Word was with God, and the Word was God"* (John 1:1 NIV). God's Word is divinely inspired and all about who God is, how much He loves us, how we should live, and what to expect in the future. So open up the Book of Life every day and bask in it. I like what Psalms 119:18 says: *"Open my eyes that I may see wonderful things in your law."*

- **Be faithful in church**: Find a Bible-believing, Christ-honoring church and plant your life there. They say the average church member goes to church once or twice a month. Don't be average; be active. Be available and an asset in your church. Discover your spiritual giftedness and serve in the church. Don't just be a pew warmer—get your hands dirty and do what God has made you to do. This is the true form of fulfillment and purpose. There are way too many Christians who are just spectators and not participants. All Christians have at least one spiritual gift and they should use it for His glory in the church. Thom S. Rainer wrote a great book entitled *I Am a Church Member*. Here's an excerpt from it:

  > **This membership is a gift. When I received the free gift of salvation through Jesus Christ, I became a part of the body of Christ. I soon thereafter**

identified with a local body and was baptized. And now I am humbled and honored to serve and to love others in our church. I pray that I will never take my membership for granted, but see it as a gift and an opportunity to serve others and to be a part of something so much greater than any one person or member.[4]

But you, man of God, flee from all this,
and pursue righteousness, godliness, faith,
love, endurance and gentleness.

1 Timothy 6:11

Photo by: Ben White on Unsplash

Chapter 3

BE THE LEADER

THE BEST LEADER is a servant leader. Jesus was a servant leader. He didn't just *tell* how to lead, but He *demonstrated* how to lead. Some leaders serve themselves, but servant leaders serve others. Servant leaders are always looking for ways to serve others. They are focused on Jesus. When someone is focused on Jesus, he will inevitably look for opportunities to serve others.

Every married couple is looking for a good marriage to follow and watch. Every married couple should have mentors to help, assist, and give advice. Why don't you *be* that married couple that mentors. Be a leader for marriages. Be the husband and wife that exemplifies Christ and His church. Be the husband and wife that encourages and motivates other marriages. In this way you are being servant leaders. You are serving other marriages.

Men, you are called by God to be the spiritual leader of the family. A great start is to fall in love with God and then love your wife by serving her. That's exactly what Jesus did. He served us by laying down His life for us so that we might have life—abundant and eternal.

Serve your wife and family by providing for them and protecting them. Provide food, shelter, and clothing for your family. This also means you should help with the cooking and cleaning of the food, fixing broken things around the house, and washing and folding those clothes too. (You're welcome ladies). Find out God's will for your career and put your passions and abilities to work to earn a living. Protect them physically, mentally, psychologically, and spiritually. Be strong physically and protect your family from people that may want to harm them. Be in the best shape possible. A good rule of thumb is to make sure your chest sticks out farther than your gut. This is quite a battle for many of us. I have to do a full body workout 2-3 times a week and cardio every day in order to maintain and stay in decent shape.

Also, protect your family mentally by guarding their eyes and minds by filtering what comes in your house via television and the internet. Protect your family psychologically by spending quality and quantity time with them. Fathers have such a huge role in the psychological makeup of their children. Being a loving and gracious husband and father builds so much **security** in the rest of the family members. Protect your family spiritually by leading them and being a role model for Christ. Tell them about the Gospel and how God changed your life. Teach them the Word by leading family devotions and praying for and with each of them. Bring your family to church. Don't make them bring you. Be the one to say like Joshua did, "*as for me and my household, we will serve the Lord*" (Joshua 24:15 NIV).

Dr. Johnny Hunt always says, "A reader is a leader and a leader is a reader." So if you want to be an effective spiritual leader, you must read. Read the Bible. Read godly books on marriage, parenting, leadership, etc. I've always heard that most men do not read a book out of high school. Yet, we can read the ticker on ESPN for hours. We need to fill our brains and hearts with *wisdom* that is going to *help* us.

As a pastor and men's ministry leader, I have led men through the 3-book series, *Every Man a Warrior*, by Lonnie Berger. It is an excellent resource on becoming the spiritual leader. Here's what Berger said in book 1:

> **As Christian men we are constantly engaged in a war. Whether we realize it or not, our life is the battlefield and Satan is our enemy. When you accept and know Christ, the battle is on. Now you are a threat to Satan's kingdom and he begins to fight. The more you grow in Christ, the brighter your light pierces through Satan's veil of darkness. The Enemy is exposed; your joy is attractive to others. The Devil must work to discredit you.[5]**

As leaders, we must be ready for the battle, and many times it's a battle for the brain. That is why it is so important to renew our minds with the Word of God. We must discipline ourselves for the purpose of godliness. We must put on the full armor of God and stand against the evil one. We must be intentional about our good intentions and be the leader God has called us to be.

Read part of Caleb's story below on how God used his wife to help him become the spiritual leader:

> **My testimony is that I failed my wife, Emily, early on even while we were dating by not being the spiritual leader in our relationship. God used that sweet girl to bring my life back into His will. We were married on June 5, 2010; and have been married for 10 years now. We have three**

beautiful children, Cooper, Eden, and Liza Jane, whom we love very much. Because of Emily's witness in my life I was able to seek God's will. I changed my major from Education and Coaching to Criminal Justice. God has called me to a life in Law Enforcement and I have an extreme passion for it. This job allows my wife to be at home with our children, which is such a blessing. God sent me that 4'11", blonde hair, green eyed, Mississippi State Bulldog's cheerleader, and used her to show me what it meant to be the spiritual leader. I strive to be the man that the Lord wants me to be every day now.

Wives, submit yourselves to your own husbands as you do to the Lord. For the husband is the head of the wife as Christ is the head of the church, his body, of which he is the Savior.

Ephesians 5:22–23

Photo by: Ben White on Unsplash

Chapter 4
BE THE LADY

WHAT IS A lady anyway? A lady has manners, doesn't use foul or vulgar language, dresses tastefully and modestly (also dresses like a woman and not a man), isn't loud and boisterous, is gracious and kind, is polite and sociable, isn't jealous and a gossip (many times people gossip because they are jealous), is secure and stable, has a gentle and quiet spirit, is hospitable and generous, is proper and level-headed, doesn't have a temper, is well groomed, has a great attitude, takes care of her body, is honest and trustworthy, is clean, is feminine, gets to know people instead of talking about herself all the time, doesn't flaunt, has standards, is a great listener and conversationalist, knows who she is in Christ, respects her elders, honors her parents and her husband, nurtures her children, is fun and joyful, and is humble and teachable.

Wow, that's quite a run-on sentence and a huge list that seems impossible to live up to. Well, it's a process. The question is, "Are you *in* the process?" Some women just give up because they feel defeated. This Proverbs 31 woman/lady seems like an impossibility or Supergirl. So here's what you do. First, pray about it. Ask God to help you become the woman He wants you to be. Second, get a mentor. Find a godly lady and spend time with her. Meet with her regularly and ask lots of questions. Third, celebrate the things you do well and work on the ones where you are struggling. For example, if you are quick-tempered, listen to a sermon on anger or read a book on this. Repent and memorize scripture about anger. Then, when you become quick-tempered, speak God's word aloud. Let His word calm your spirit. Ask God to help you to have a *"gentle and quiet spirit"* (1 Peter 3:4).

Concerning her husband, a *lady* respects him, honors him, supports him, encourages him, believes in him, talks good about him, and is proud of him. A true lady really is a Proverbs 31 lady. This is hard to find. Look at what Proverbs 31:10 says: *"A wife of noble character who can find? She is worth far more than rubies."* So, a lady should read and study Proverbs 31 and apply it to her life (along with other scriptures). In return she will be respected and loved. Want proof? Look at Proverbs 31:28: *"Her children arise and call her blessed; her husband also, and he praises her."*

Have you ever seen a Proverbs 31 lady? I have. I have seen several throughout the years. They are calm, cool, and collected. You can tell they walk with God. They are well-respected and many go to them for advice. They are godly and being used of the Lord, and so can you. Just make yourself available as moldable clay. Allow the God of the universe to transform you into a Godly lady.

> *Likewise, teach the older women to be reverent in the way they live, not to be slanderers or addicted to much wine, but to teach what is good. Then they can urge the younger women to love their husbands and children, to be self-controlled and pure, to be busy at home, to be kind, and to be subject to their husbands, so that no one will malign the word of God.*

Titus 2:3–5

Photo by: John Moeses Bauan on Unsplash

Chapter 5
BE WILLING

BE WILLING MEANS "to agree freely to; not opposed to doing something; or ready or eager to do something," according to Webster. Are you "willing" to put forth the effort to make your marriage great? Remember, you can only change yourself; you can't change anyone else. So be willing to change yourself.

You should ask your spouse what they would change about you and actually listen without getting offended. Start with one or two things and not a long list. We all have quirks and idiosyncrasies that might just drive our spouse crazy.

Kari and I talk about this sometimes and here's the latest thing I *chose* to change: When I wake up in the morning, I take a shower and then make some coffee. I lay the kitchen towel out on the counter and put my cup and the sugar bowl on the towel. The towel is there to catch spilled sugar or coffee. It's preventative maintenance ... Well, apparently this drives Kari crazy because I would leave the towel there on the counter instead of putting it back on the stove handle. And so, I was willing to change and I did.

It's the little things that make a big difference. Are there little things you wish your spouse would do or not do? Why don't you gently tell him or her? Shaunti Feldhahn reports of a couple: "Shortly after their divorce one woman said, 'My husband worked so hard for a whole year to take us to Hawaii and all I wanted him to do was put his arm around me at church.'"[6] What a small thing to want and need. So be willing to do your part and change some things. Whatever your spouse wants you to change, do it. It could make a world of difference in your marriage. It could literally save your marriage.

If you are willing and obedient, you will
eat the good things of the land.

Isaiah 1:19

Chapter 6

BE GREAT

BE A GREAT spouse. Do your best to be the best wife or husband you can be for the glory of God. After reading and implementing the nuggets in this book, you are well on your way. Don't give your spouse a reason to look elsewhere. May your spouse be excited to hear the garage door open when you are coming home from work. Treat each other like kings and queens.

Here's the problem. We want our spouse to treat *us* like a king or queen. Our selfishness wants to be treated, not to be the one to treat. God knew our selfishness and gave us the power to overcome it. He gave us the Holy Spirit to help us be great for His glory. He is a part of the Trinity. The Trinity consists of God the Father, God the Son, and God the Spirit. I read Oswald Chamber's *My Utmost for His Highest* every day and here's what he said on April 12:

> **'You shall receive power when the Holy Spirit has come upon you ...' (Acts 1:8)—not power as a gift from the Holy Spirit; the power is the Holy Spirit, not something that He gives us.**[7]

Did you get it? Many times we want the *power* of the Holy Spirit when **HE** *is* the power! So, here's what the Holy Spirit does for us if we allow Him to fill us every day. This is the secret to being great. It's found in Galatians 5:22–23: "*But the fruit of the Spirit is love, joy, peace, patience, kindness, goodness, faithfulness, gentleness, and self-control …*" (NASB). When we are Spirit-led, we are more loving, joyful, peaceful, patient, kind, good (great), faithful, gentle, and controlled. Isn't that what you want your spouse to be? Isn't that what you should be if you are a believer? Be willing to be filled with the Spirit of God and keep on being filled.

Instead, whoever wants to become great
among you must be your servant.

Matthew 20:26

Photo by: Shanique Wright on Unsplash

Chapter 7

BE LOVING

THE BEST WAY to be loving is to realize how much God loves you. Check this out from 1 John 4:16–19:

> *We have come to know and have believed the love which God has for us. God is love, and the one who abides in love abides in God, and God abides in him. By this, love is perfected with us, so that we may have confidence in the day of judgment; because as He is, so also are we in this world. There is no fear in love; but perfect love casts out fear, because fear involves punishment, and the one who fears is not perfected in love. We love, because He first loved us.*

Abide in God and let God abide in you and His love will come pouring out. God's love for us gives us the confidence and power to love others without fear. Let this sink in. You can love without the fear of not being loved back. It's an unconditional love.

Remember back in Galatians 5:22? The fruit of the Spirit is what? The first thing He mentions is LOVE. So, allow the Spirit of God to love through you. When love is not reciprocated, Godly love flows through us in a mighty powerful way. The world needs to see God's love and God wants to do it—through you. The Apostle Paul tells us in Romans 5:5, *"And hope does not put us to shame, because God's love has been poured out into our hearts through the Holy Spirit, who has been given to us."*

Another way to *be loving* is to speak your spouse's love language. In 1992 Dr. Gary Chapman wrote a book entitled *The 5 Love Languages* to help couples understand that there are five emotional love languages. For the first seven years of our marriage Kari and I were trying to love each other by speaking our own love language, and it was challenging to say the least.

I purred like a cat and felt loved when she would touch me, give me a massage, or make love to me. She was happy and felt loved when I would speak kind and encouraging words to her.

Here was the problem: I was speaking my own love language to her and she was speaking her own love language to me. We were both discouraged and frustrated. I was touching her because it came naturally to me, and she was verbally encouraging me because it came naturally to her. I wanted her to touch me and she wanted me to speak kind words to her. We didn't realize this until we read Chapman's book on love languages and it made sense. This is why we must read, learn, and study about marriage to make it great and loving.

We have to *choose* to speak our spouse's love language because it doesn't come naturally to us. Here's what Chapman says in his book:

> **Once you identify and learn to speak your spouse's primary love language, I believe that you will have discovered the key to a long-lasting, loving marriage.**[8]

I want to motivate you and your spouse to take the love language test at **www.5lovelanguages.com/profile/.** After you take it, compare notes and start speaking each other's love language. When implemented consistently, it will make a world of difference in your marriage. Also, it will help you be a better parent too when you discover your children's love languages.

Jesus replied: 'Love the Lord your God with all your heart and with all your soul and with all your mind.' This is the first and greatest commandment. And the second is like it: 'Love your neighbor as yourself.' All the Law and the Prophets hang on these two commandments.

Matthew 22:37–40

Photo by: Carly Rae Hobbins on Unsplash

Chapter 8

BE DETERMINED

BE DETERMINED TO have a loving, growing marriage no matter what. Jake and Lincoln have been through some life-and-death trials early on in their marriage. Here is their story and the secret of determination:

> Our loving Father has sharpened our marriage through a couple of recent battles that might have otherwise crushed us had we not turned to our faithful God. After welcoming our first child, Wyatt, into the world in October of 2015, Jake went to the police academy in January of 2016. Despite his preparatory training, Jake came home with complete kidney failure at 23 years of age. During this time, God gave me a complete peace that He would work everything for our good. Never once did I believe that Jake would not have a full recovery. Out of the ten days Jake spent in the hospital, I recall one day where I let Satan creep in and make me feel sorry for myself. On my way home from the hospital that day, a song came on the radio called "Just Be Held" by Casting Crowns. The Lord spoke to me through every lyric, but one part stuck with me that night: "Your world's not falling apart, it's falling into place/

I'm on the throne, stop holding on and just be held."

Praise the Lord for His healing and willingness to hold us no matter our sins and faults! Jake completely recovered and is now a federal probation officer. Our second battle began about two months later in March of 2016. Our son, Wyatt, now five years old, suddenly began to get very weak and stopped eating. After taking him to his pediatrician and the emergency room, Wyatt showed no signs of bacterial infections and his blood work was normal. A day later, we saw his pediatrician again because Wyatt was getting worse. We were then sent to Le Bonheur Children's Hospital in Memphis, TN, with suspicions of botulism. Infantile botulism is a rare disease that is mostly associated with infants consuming honey or home-canned foods. Wyatt spent ten days in the hospital and received an antitoxin for treatment of botulism. The night before we went home, we got the results back that confirmed Wyatt had infantile botulism. We are still uncertain what caused Wyatt to suffer this rare disease, but God healed our baby!

What a testimony God has blessed our family with! We are anxious to share this testimony with Wyatt! Jake and I grew closer in the Lord during these trials through prayer and professions of our faith. God does not have to give us reasons why we go through storms in life. Jake and I have been married for seven years, but our encouragement to other couples that are facing storms or who are ready to give up is to look to the Lord. Another stanza of the song mentioned above sums up our experience and God's promise: "If your eyes are on the storm/ You'll wonder if I love you still/ But if your eyes are on the cross/ You'll know I always have and I always will." We serve a healing God and He will see you through.

Just like Jake and Lincoln, be determined to press on in the Lord no matter what comes your way.

Brothers and sisters, I do not consider myself yet to have taken hold of it. But one thing I do: Forgetting what is behind and straining toward what is ahead, I press on toward the goal to win the prize for which God has called me heavenward in Christ Jesus.

Philippians 3:13–14

Chapter 9
BE FAITHFUL

TO BE FAITHFUL means to be loyal, dependable, trustworthy, and committed. Most of us said words like this to each other at our wedding in front of God, family, and friends. However, if you watch much television or many movies you will see this being thrown out the window. Most of the time television and movies do not show the negative repercussions of unfaithfulness.

Most of the time unfaithfulness in marriage leads to divorce. It doesn't have to, but most of the time it does. And when it does, there is another list of issues you have to deal with. I'll just list a few potential repercussions of divorce:

- Unforgiveness
- Bitterness
- Depression
- Shame
- Financial woes
- Insecurity
- Anger
- Custody over children
- Children's insecurity, blame, unforgiveness, etc.

So, let's do some preventative maintenance so as not to succumb to unfaithfulness. Here is a list of ways to remain faithful:

- Implement this book.
- Fall in love with God.
- Pursue your spouse.
- Date your spouse.
- Keep the home fires burning. Fan the flame of passion.
- Don't talk about intimate issues with the other gender.
- Don't let your eyes wander and linger (Hebrews 12:2).
- Don't look at pornography or watch sensual movies or TV shows.
- Don't let your thoughts wander (2 Corinthians 10:5).
- Don't give the opposite gender a ride in your car alone.
- Spend more time with your spouse.
- Run from temptation like Joseph did (Genesis 39:12).
- Avoid looking up old girlfriends and boyfriends.
- Don't be with the other gender behind a closed door.
- Don't flirt with others. Continue to flirt with your spouse.
- Get a filter for your computer and phone and give your spouse the password.
- Work all arguments out or go to a Christian counselor.
- Avoid being separated from your spouse very much.
- Never go on a business trip with the opposite gender. Take your spouse with you if at all possible.
- Forgive.

I am sure there are many more things to do to remain faithful, but this is a good start. Be faithful to God, your spouse, and your children. Learn what I do to be faithful in chapter 27.

You have heard that it was said, 'You shall not commit adultery.'
But I tell you that anyone who looks at a woman lustfully
has already committed adultery with her in his heart.

Matthew 5:27–28

Chapter 10
BE ATTENTIVE

BEING ATTENTIVE IS becoming harder to do with all of the distractions these days. It seems like there is a monitor/screen to look at everywhere you go. There are so many things that are screaming for your attention that it's hard to focus, especially if you have A.D.D. like me. One of the worst places to take your wife on a date is at a restaurant filled with television screens. Don't even try, guys. You will not give your wife the attention she needs and deserves.

Being attentive means to be perceptive, alert, and aware. I'm thinking of a tennis ball boy or girl, and how attentive they must be during a tennis match. They have to be quick to respond when a ball hits the net or when a player needs a ball. We should be as attentive to our spouse's needs, wants, and desires—always ready to serve. Kari longs for me to pay attention to her and to notice her. We've been married for more than 23 years and we still need to catch each other's eyes.

Be an attentive spouse by listening with your ears, looking with your eyes, responding with your mouth, and using body language. Don't look at your phone or the television while trying to listen. Give them your undivided attention. Guys, our wives do not always want solutions either, they just want us to listen and care. Start to-day by being attentive to your spouse. Look at them more often. Notice them more often. Ladies, on a side note, don't expect your husband to be a good listener if you are taking a bath in front of him and trying to have a conversation. He *will* be distracted with your naked body. *"A man's eyes are never satisfied"* (Proverbs 27:20).

To answer before listening—that is folly and shame.

Proverbs 18:13

Chapter 11
BE PATIENT

MY PARENTS HAVE been married for over 56 years. I would say it takes patience to be married that long. Patience is a fruit of the Spirit. It helps in any relationship. Do you remember the old expression, "Don't get your trousers in a twist?" In other words, be patient; relax.

My dad is one of the most patient men that I know. He has rested and trusted in the Lord throughout his life and it shows.

My parents submitted these nuggets of wisdom on marriage after 56 years of patience:

- A couple must have a strong faith in God and a desire to obey His word.
- A husband should be a leader in his household, and in order to lead you must first be a follower. A husband should follow God and seek His guidance so that he can lead his family in God's will.
- Never argue in front of your children or use an argumentative tone to instruct your children.
- It is important to find a couple from whom to seek

guidance—one that is rooted in God's Word.

- Realize no marriage is perfect. It is give and take from both sides. You have to resolve that you are going to work to make your marriage work. Don't be selfish.
- Take out a joint bank account and discuss how money will be spent. After preparing a budget together, follow it. If a discrepancy occurs and a decision must be made or action taken, the husband should take the lead and accept the responsibility.
- Express to your mate often your love and need for him or her. Appreciate their weaknesses and the way that your weaknesses are filled and made strong by your marriage.

All of these nuggets take patience. So pursue patience and learn from others who have gone before you. My parents have had disagreements but have been patient and have left a legacy for me and my siblings, Mike and Anita.

Whoever is patient has great understanding,
but one who is quick-tempered displays folly.

Proverbs 14:29

Photo by: AllGo on Unsplash

Chapter 12

BE SELFLESS

HAVE YOU EVER thought, *if everyone on earth were born-again believers this world would be so much better?* The same is true that if everyone were selfless, the world would be so much better. Jesus is our only perfect example here. Philippians 2:5–7 tells us, *"In your relationships with one another, have the same mindset as Christ Jesus: Who, being in very nature God, did not consider equality with God something to be used to His own advantage; rather, He made Himself nothing by taking the very nature of a servant, being made in human likeness."*

Jesus was the epitome of selflessness. He could have stayed in Heaven in His glorious deity yet He came to be our selfless Savior. Being selfless is a lifelong pursuit because of our sinful nature. The sinful nature has at the root the terms *me, myself,* and *I.* Many people get married to fulfill "their" own desires.

I recently counseled a husband on the brink of divorce and I asked him, "If you could sum it up, what is the one reason you are pursuing a divorce?" He said, "She doesn't make me happy." I told him that is the wrong approach and outlook. We should *long* to make our spouse happy. Selflessness has the power to make your marriage amazing!

Ask your spouse today, "How can I make *you* happy?" When your spouse realizes that you are trying to make them happy, they might just try their best to make *you* happy. Here is a verse we should put on our bathroom mirror or on our refrigerator to live by:

> **Do nothing from selfishness or empty conceit, but with humility of mind regard one another as more important than yourselves; do not merely look out for your own personal interests, but also for the interests of others. (Philippians 2:3–4 NASB)**

Selfishness is one of the main reasons for divorce. It's strange that while you are dating your future spouse you will do anything to please them and make them happy, but once you get married your focus goes back to YOU. Of course it doesn't have to be this way. All you have to do is humble yourself like Jesus did and realize life is not about you. It is about Jesus, others, and then yourself. That is the true meaning of joy (J > Jesus, O > Others, Y > Yourself).

> **Do to others as you would have them do to you.**

> **Luke 6:31**

Photo by: Anthony Tran on Unsplash

Chapter 13
BE FORGIVING

FORGIVENESS IS THE key to Christianity. The Apostle Paul tells us in Ephesians 4:32, *"Be kind and compassionate to one another, forgiving each other, just as in Christ God forgave you"* (NIV). In marriage, it is inevitable that we are going to hurt, upset, or disappoint each other. The question is: What do we do about it? Here's how Dr. John Townsend addresses this in his book *Rescue Your Love Life*:

> There are only two ways to relate to each other: through the law and through forgiveness. No third alternative exists. When one of you is selfish, irresponsible, or hurtful, you can choose one of these two paths. The first path is to extract an eye for an eye, insisting that a debt must be paid. In relationships, this means partners keep a scorecard of hurts and transgressions. They withdraw love and empathy until they've gotten justice, revenge, or both. And no relationship can sustain that amount of law. The connection goes away, and the relationship often just dies.
>
> Forgiveness, the other path, is the only hope. When one partner incurs the debt, the other feels the pain and knows

she has been wronged. But she lets go of her right to demand justice. She lets the prisoner go free, so to speak.[9]

Forgiveness can be very difficult but highly necessary for you, your sanity, and state of mind. Joyce Meyer, in her article "The Poison of Unforgiveness," says: "Many people ruin their health and their lives by taking the poison of bitterness, resentment, and unforgiveness." She goes on to say:

Who are you helping most when you forgive the person who hurt you? Actually, you're helping yourself more than the other person. I always looked at forgiving people who hurt me as being really hard. I thought it seemed so unfair for them to receive forgiveness when I had gotten hurt. I got pain, and they got freedom without having to pay for the pain they caused. Now I realize that I'm helping myself when I choose to forgive.[10]

Forgiveness is a beautiful thing—literally. Your face lights up when you forgive. I know someone who has much unforgiveness in her and I can see it in her face. Unforgiveness will stress you out, and we all know what stress does to someone. Or do you? I'll enlighten you. It's common knowledge that stress can cause anxiety, headaches, fatigue, sleep problems, irritability, sadness, anger, depression, restlessness, stomachache, muscle pain, etc. Spouses need to learn to say, "I'm sorry, will you forgive me?" "Yes, I will forgive you." If God can forgive us, we can forgive others.

Unforgiveness is a slippery slope. I believe that unforgiveness breeds bitterness, bitterness breeds depression, and depression breeds suicide. That's a pretty steep slippery slope. You can avoid this slope by forgiving. The Holy Spirit of God can help you. Let Him, and feel the freedom.

But if you do not forgive others their sins,
your Father will not forgive your sins.

Matthew 6:15

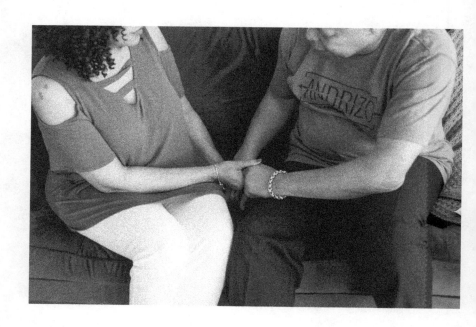

Chapter 14
BE PRAYED UP

YOU'VE HEARD IT said, "Those that pray together, stay together." "The divorce rate of couples that pray together is about one in ten thousand,"[11] according to Dr. Phil in his book *Relationship Rescue*. There is something that is so bonding about praying together. Praying together just connects you to each other.

Not only should we pray together, we should pray by ourselves. We have to be intentional about praying. Proverbs 3:6 tells us, "*In all your ways acknowledge Him, and He shall direct your paths*" (NKJV). We need to talk to God about everything. He is intimately interested in all of our ways. So we shouldn't just pray about the big things in our lives, we should pray about the little things as well.

We should pray about our marriage quite often, asking God to put a hedge of protection around it. The devil doesn't like you or your marriage. He wants to destroy your marriage so we have to be prayed up. Ask God to strengthen and grow your marriage to complete oneness for His glory. Ask God to help your marriage to be a witness and a role model for others to see the Gospel as God being the bridegroom and the church being the bride.

Oswald Chambers said in his devotional, *My Utmost for His Highest*, "Prayer does not equip us for greater works - prayer is the great work."[12] Prayer is work. Have you ever tried to pray without asking God for anything? It's very difficult. Our prayer life should mature to the point of wanting to become one with God instead of asking him for things all the time. Little kids ask their parents for things all the time. When those kids become *mature* adults, they just want to be with their parents and enjoy their presence.

Prayer connects us to God and God connects us to purpose and fulfillment. As a couple, connect with God, Who is *for* your marriage, and allow Him to fortify your unity. Commit to pray together every day, in addition to praying at mealtimes.

Rejoice always, pray continually, give thanks in all circumstances; for this is God's will for you in Christ Jesus.

1 Thessalonians 5:16–18

Photo by: Naassom Azevedo on Unsplash

Chapter 15
BE SOLD OUT

I'M NOT REALLY talking about marriage here. I'm talking about being sold out to the Lord. Would someone describe you as being "sold out to Christ"? Being sold out to Christ will inevitably strengthen your marriage—remember the "triangle effect" in chapter 2?

Being sold out to Christ means you are committed to obey despite the cost. It means to honor Christ with the life He's given you. It means to delight yourself in the Lord. It means to daily be *"dead to self and alive to God"* (Romans 6:11). Being *alive to God* means to be Spirit filled or filled with the Spirit. Every day we should ask the Lord to fill us with His Spirit and anoint us to carry out His will for our lives to honor and glorify Him. It is a constant filling of His Spirit. Yes, once we are saved, God places His Spirit within us and He will never leave us but we quench the Spirit so often. We need a continuous flow of His Spirit for Him to flow *through* us like an open vessel. *"It is Christ in me, the hope of glory"* (Colossians 1:27b).

Many years ago I served at First Baptist Church Woodstock as the Assimilation Pastor, and their vision was to worship God, love others, serve God, and invite others. That is what a sold-out person does. They *worship God* throughout the week and not just on

Sundays. They *love others* by being in a small group/life group/ Connect group/SS class/home group or whatever you want to call it, fellowshipping, and studying the Bible together. A sold-out person *serves God* within their spiritual giftedness to fortify the church. And a sold-out person *invites others* to church and to Christ and starts with their relatives, neighbors, work associates, and friends.

But whatever were gains to me I now consider loss for the sake of Christ. What is more, I consider everything a loss because of the surpassing worth of knowing Christ Jesus my Lord, for whose sake I have lost all things. I consider them garbage, that I may gain Christ and be found in him, not having a righteousness of my own that comes from the law, but that which is through faith in Christ - the righteousness that comes from God on the basis of faith. I want to know Christ - yes, to know the power of his resurrection and participation in his sufferings, becoming like him in his death.

Philippians 3:7–10

Chapter 16
BE ROMANTIC

THE INFORMAL DEFINITION of romance is "to court or woo romantically; treat with ardor or chivalrousness." Another definition is "to invent or relate romances; indulge in fanciful or extravagant stories or daydreams."[13] Most people have romantic fantasies and come into marriage assuming their spouse will fulfill them. The strange thing is that many spouses never communicate those romantic desires with their partner. All this does is promote frustration and disappointment.

I recommend that you share your romantic wishes with your spouse. I also recommend that you ask your spouse what their romantic ideas are and then fulfill them (unless they make you feel uncomfortable). Have fun with this. Make fun memories. Schedule it and have fun.

I got ahead of myself. There has to be kindness and gentleness shown. There has to be continuous flirting involved. We need to look our best for each other and respect each other. We need to act like we did when we were dating each other, showing each other a ton of attention. Looking into our spouse's eyes, holding hands, hugging, kissing, opening the car door, writing notes to each other, saying "I miss you" and "I love you," giving each other massages, giving her flowers, cooking his favorite meal, surprising each other at work with a gift or special lunch, planning a date night, break out the candles and a little mood music, carve your initials in a tree, spit off a bridge, etc.

In writing this just now, I sent my wife an e-mail and attached Barry White's song "Can't Get Enough of Your Love, Babe." I said in the subject: "This is the way I feel about you." I'm trying to be romantic and implement what I write. I'll let you know later if it worked. Wait a minute—that's not the right motive! We should be romantic because we love our spouses and want to show it, not to get anything in return.

So how can you be more romantic? The best way is to ask your spouse. Just ask them, "How can I be more romantic?" Ask them to write down ways you can be more romantic and then find the right time to do them. Communication solves so many things in marriage. We can't read each other's minds so open your mouth (in a kind and gentle way).

How beautiful you are, my darling!
Oh, how beautiful!
Your eyes are doves.

How handsome you are, my beloved!
Oh, how charming!
And our bed is verdant.

Song of Solomon 1:15–16

Chapter 17
BE SEXY

ANYONE CAN BE sexy, no matter how you think you look. Husbands and wives should look for ways to be sexy for each other. This is the sugar and spice of marriage that should never end. For some reason I am thinking of Pepé Le Pew from *Looney Tunes*. He was always in a sexy mood and full of love and romance. Couples should never let the embers cool down but stay hot towards each other.

In my previous book, *Top 10 Components of a Strong Marriage*, there was a chapter entitled "Dress Classy in Public and Sexy in Private." In that chapter, I was speaking to women and said, "You don't have to dress sexy every night." Even though your husband would really like for his new bride to dress sexy every night of the honeymoon and at least once a week throughout the first year. So, as much as possible, most men want their wives to be sexy and frisky (you like that word?). The key to this is to communicate and compromise.

Women do not have to wear lingerie to be sexy. You could wear your husband's button-down and be sexy. You could wear your bathrobe and be sexy. Or you could wear your birthday suit and be sexy. I tell Kari that she would look great in a sackcloth. There are many ways to dress sexy. Have fun with this. Pick out clothes for each other sometimes and *strut your stuff.*

I know what you are thinking: "Being sexy doesn't just involve how you dress." I know. Being sexy involves making eye contact, smiling, having an upbeat attitude, having a healthy body, having a good sense of humor and personality, smelling good, being clean, painting your nails, wearing makeup, having the house in order, fixing your hair (having your hair fixed affects your mood and confidence), touching, and being in shape makes you feel sexy. Ladies, the sexiest thing you can do for your husband is to desire him sexually ... period.

Guys, you should ask your wife how *you* can be sexy too. Some ways men can be sexy include: being confident but not arrogant, being manly, working hard, doesn't mind getting dirty, gets a job done, is attentive to his bride, being clean, smelling good, well groomed (nails clipped, nose and ear hairs removed, clean hair, remove oil and dandruff), brushes his teeth, has a great attitude, is strong, protects his family, is the spiritual leader, helps with the kids and house, communicates and listens, doesn't swear and has a good sense of humor. Men, the sexiest thing you can do for your wife is to give her security and attention.

Couples should be able to be sexy without rejection. We need to always compliment each other's sexiness. In marriage, we should have the freedom to be sexy without any insecurity. Even if you don't necessarily like your body, you can be sexy because your spouse *chose* you, *loves* you, and *wants* you to be sexy. How many times can I say "*sexy*"? To the husband and wife, be classy in public and sexy in private. Enjoy each other.

All night long on my bed I looked for the one my heart loves.

Song of Solomon 3:1

Photo by: Becca Tapert on Unsplash

Chapter 18
BE AVAILABLE

IN OUR MEDIA-DRIVEN world you would think that being available would be easy. Yes, with the use of cell phones and computers, we can connect with anyone within seconds just about anywhere in the world. And we have the privilege to see who is trying to connect with us and have the choice to answer or not. While a preacher was preaching one time, someone's phone rang and the preacher said, "Unless that's God calling, please don't answer it."

We should always be available to our spouses when they need us. My wife has an understood permission to come in my office at any time—even if I am in a meeting. She has the freedom to call or text me at any time. I usually let her know when I'm in a meeting and I can't answer, though. She even has the freedom to wake me up in the middle of the night to tell me she heard something in the house and for me to go check it out.

Our spouses should take precedence over everyone except God. Our priorities should be God, spouse, children, other family members, and then everyone else. Yes, we should give each other space, but we should be freely accessible to our spouses. If we are not available to our spouse, you might find yourself *available*. That's a sad play-on-words but there is a lot of truth in it.

Spouses have to be very cautious about being too busy with everything else except for their mate. This can be easy to do. You have to learn to say "no" to some things. If the devil can't make you bad, he'll make you busy. If you haven't been on a date with your spouse in 3 months, you are too busy. If you haven't been on a one- or two-night getaway in a year, you are too busy. If you haven't sat down for supper in your house in a month, you're too busy.

A great marriage takes work, consistency, and intentionality. Be available to your spouse to help each other, to hold each other, to make love, to have a date, to have children, to get away, to dream together, to talk about the day, to set goals, to go to a marriage class or retreat, to pray together, to go to your class reunions, to ride bikes, etc. One of the best things couples should do when they come home from work is to take 5–10 minutes and talk about their day. Be available to connect.

Rejoice with those who rejoice; mourn with those who mourn.

Romans 12:15

Photo by: Esther Ann on Unsplash

Chapter 19
BE GENTLE

COUPLES MUST BE gentle with each other in their tone and language. We shouldn't be harsh or rude. A good rule of thumb is to never raise your voice towards your spouse. You CAN control your voice. Choose not to scream and yell. It really doesn't help matters. I'm sure your spouse can hear just fine, so no need to yell. If you yell at your spouse a lot, eventually they will avoid you. Who wants to be yelled at a lot? So, show some maturity and keep your voice down when having a *discussion*.

Husbands should be gentle with their wives as they are the *weaker vessel*. Of course some wives are stronger than their husbands, but most are not. 1 Peter 3:7 Paul states, "*You husbands in the same way, live with your wives in an understanding way, as with someone weaker, since she is a woman; and show her honor as a fellow heir of the grace of life, so that your prayers will not be hindered*" (NASB).

Honor each other like kings and queens. Be gentle and handle each other with care like they are a million-dollar vase. Ask each other, "Am I gentle?"

Let your gentleness be evident to all. The Lord is near.
Philippians 4:5

Photo by: Jared Sluyter on Unsplash

Chapter 20
BE FUN

I LOVE TO have fun. When we realize that we are not in charge of the world and can trust God in all things, we can relax and have fun. Life is fun. You really *can have* an abundant life. *"The joy of the Lord is your strength."* (Nehemiah 8:10) God has this. I love what Jesus tells us in John 16:33: *"These things I have spoken to you, that in Me you may have peace. In the world you will have tribulation; but be of good cheer, I have overcome the world"* (NKJV). Just walk with God and enjoy life, even in the dark times and seasons.

Don't let go of the unseen hand of God. Trust that He is up to something good. God has a purpose and a plan for your life. Bad things happen for many reasons. Sometimes God is increasing our faith. Sometimes He wants to connect us with someone to share the Gospel. Sometimes He is teaching us something new. Sometimes He allows us to go through things because He wants to use us to encourage others who will go through the same thing one day. Walk with God, not ahead of or behind Him. It's fun to walk with God because He is fun. Remember, He created a sense of humor.

Don't you love being around a "fun" person? Life is too short to take it too seriously. Learn to laugh at yourself. Ted Cunningham, in his book, *Fun Loving You,* said this:

> **Not taking yourself so seriously is the first step toward bringing laughter into your marriage. Being a responsible adult does not mean that you must remain serious at all times. Self-deprecating humor goes a long way in building intimacy in your marriage. God wants you to laugh.**[14]

Every couple should have fun together. When the children come it seems that life gets real serious because you are responsible for them and now you have to figure out how to be a good parent, let alone a good husband or wife. *Enjoy* your children; don't just *endure* them. Now that's a good word. Even though you have more responsibility when the children come, you can still have lots of fun.

Brainstorm with each other and figure out how to have more fun together. Life can get in a rut, and we need to dig our way out with fun and laughter. Proverbs 17:22 says, *"A cheerful heart brings good healing ..."* (NET). So how can you have fun? For us, we do a number of things. One time we went to The Comedy Barn Theater in Pigeon Forge, TN, and had a blast. We've seen Tim Hawkins in concert many times and we laugh until our bellies ache. We watch *America's Funniest Home Videos* and other things, just to laugh.

There are many other comedians to listen to and watch, but the easiest thing to do is to hang out with fun-loving people with good attitudes on life. One of the greatest places to find these types of people is in the church. We have met some of the best people in the world at church and have had a blast with them. There is a verse in 1 Corinthians 15:33 that says, *"Bad company corrupts good morals."* So be careful whom you hang around—it can affect your attitude.

Another way to have fun is to play games or sports together. Go bowling, play cards, play basketball, play coed softball, play tennis, play Apples to Apples, play Monopoly, play Life, play strip poker (wait, what?), go ice or roller skating, go hiking or biking, etc. I'm positive you and your spouse can find something that both of you can enjoy and have fun.

This is what I have observed to be good: that it is appropriate for a person to eat, to drink and to find satisfaction in their toilsome labor under the sun during the few days of life God has given them - for this is their lot. Moreover, when God gives someone wealth and possessions, and the ability to enjoy them, to accept their lot and be happy in their toil - this is a gift of God. They seldom reflect on the days of their life, because God keeps them occupied with gladness of heart.

Ecclesiastes 5:18–20

Photo by: Suzana Sousa on Unsplash

Chapter 21
BE HAPPY

IF YOU ASKED most single people "What would make you happy?" most of them would say, "It would make me happy to meet the love of my life." Many people get married to be happy. Did you get that? Many think that getting married will make them happy. However, happy people make marriage happy. You can't depend on someone else to make you happy. You have to be happy with who you are. God doesn't make junk. You are the apple of His eye. Psalms 139:14 says it best: *"I will give thanks to You, for I am fearfully and wonderfully made; wonderful are Your works, and my soul knows it very well"* (NASB).

We have so many reasons to be happy, but the least little thing can spoil our happiness. I said it "can," not that it "will." You see happiness is a choice. You must choose to be happy. You are in charge of your feelings and your thoughts, so choose to be happy. Dwell on the happy things in your life instead of things that do not make you happy. Some people are just looking for a reason to be unhappy and then hang out with unhappy people because misery loves company. That's no fun.

Psalms 144:15b tells us, *"How blessed (happy) are the people whose*

God is the Lord" (NASB). When God is the Lord of your life, you are a truly happy person. You are delighted and glad when you let go and let God do what He wants in your life. Many people see God with His arms crossed, but the right perspective is to see Him with His arms open to embrace you. The giver of life wants to give you a happy life. Sure, there are times of sadness and mourning, but the general makeup of your life should be happiness.

So what is robbing us of our happiness? Well, there are many things but I'll mention a few. The biggest thief is the empty soul. We all have this longing or void in our hearts that only God can fill. God wants to fill it with His Spirit. Believing and receiving that Jesus came to earth, died in our stead, and rose from the grave will satisfy that longing. When we accept what Jesus did for us on the cross, taking the punishment that we deserved, our emptiness is filled. This is the beginning of everlasting happiness.

Another thief of happiness is unforgiveness. We discussed this in chapter 13. You can see unforgiveness on someone's face if you look long enough. Another thief is dissatisfaction of yourself. Many people are not happy with the way they look. If you can do something about it, then DO IT and stop whining about it. I didn't like my teeth and so I bought my own braces when I graduated from college. I didn't like my uni-brow, so I plucked the hairs between my eyes. I didn't like the shape of my body and so I began to eat healthy and exercise.

Another thief of happiness is hanging out with the wrong crowd. You tend to act like those you hang around. So, if the people you hang out with are pulling you away from God and His Word, then stop hanging out with them. They are stealing your happiness.

One more thief I would like to mention is working in the wrong job.

You are supposed to like/love your job because that is what you were born to do. Discover your passions, talents, and spiritual giftedness and align them with a job/career. Then you will *want* to go to work because it is your purpose (see Jeremiah 29:11).

I know that there is nothing better for people than to be happy and to do good while they live.

Ecclesiastes 3:12

Photo by: Henri Pham on Unsplash

Chapter 22
BE THOUGHTFUL

THE GREATEST VERSE on this is found in Luke 6:31 when Jesus says, *"Treat others the same way you want them to treat you"* (NASB). If we could just implement this verse our marriages would be off the charts. We need to be thoughtful in our words and in our actions. In our words, we need to be consistent and courteous. Just simply saying "Please" and "Thank You" is a good start. Here's a list of thoughtful things we should say to our spouses:

- You look great today.
- I love you.
- I'm so glad I married you.
- I'm sorry.
- Please forgive me.
- How can I serve you today?
- What can I do to help?
- Our kids are lucky to have a mom/dad like you.
- I'm so proud of you.
- Being your wife is an honor.
- I'm yours.
- It's fun to work with you.
- You make me a better person.

- You are so hot.
- I wish we could've met earlier in life.

Now that's just a few. I'm sure you can come up with many more. Just say things that you would want said to you. A great thing to do is to verbally notice your spouse's accomplishments. Such as, tell your husband "the yard looks great" after he mowed it. Or tell your wife, "You are a great decorator." This is extremely important if your spouse's love language is *words of affirmation*.

In addition to *saying* thoughtful things, we should *do* thoughtful things. This also is extremely important if your spouse's love language is *acts of service*. Here is a short list of thoughtful things you can do for your spouse:

- Give her the remote
- Give a massage
- Give a massage without *strings* attached
- Open the car door (or any door) for her
- Cook his favorite dinner
- Give unexpected sex
- Give flowers
- Buy her favorite ice cream
- Write a note
- Iron all his button-downs
- Vacuum the whole house
- Buy her jewelry for no reason
- Go to the ball game with him
- Plan a date night

Of course there are a million things to do for each other. The key is to find out what they like and do that for them. We should never stop studying and pursuing each other. Because of our selfishness, we sometimes stop saying nice things or doing nice things for our mate. This is usually because they have stopped saying or doing nice things for us. Well someone has to be more mature and crank the thoughtfulness back up. In general, the more thoughtful things you say or do for your mate, the more things they will say or do for you.

In your relationships with one another,
have the same mindset as Christ Jesus:

Philippians 2:5

Photo by: Shawnee D on Unsplash

Chapter 23

BE PEACEFUL

THIS IS A saying I've heard my dad and uncles say my whole life: "Be peaceful." It's just one of those random statements they would make when they walked in the room or if someone got in an argument or scuffle. Being peaceful means to stop the chaos or commotion. It means to be at ease. Being peaceful means not getting flustered so easily—to have a long fuse. We shouldn't be so quick to get angry.

A great way to explain a peaceful person is that they are calm, cool, and collected. Peace is a fruit of the spirit in Galatians 5:22—love, joy, *peace* … Love and joy together produce peace. Agape love brings joy to the soul, which produces peace. Peace goes hand-in-hand with faith. By having peace, we can sustain anything, knowing that God is in control.

Do you have a peaceful marriage? What can you do to instigate peace in your marriage? Maybe you need to take a different approach to something you do not like that your spouse does. Once again, you can only change "you." The greatest way to bring more peace in your marriage is to pray specifically about the problem. Pray by yourself and then pray with your spouse about it and let

God give you answers. Also, seek His Word about the problem. The Word of God may speak directly to the problem or may give principles to help the problem. Lastly, seek wise counsel from a godly mentor or Christian counselor.

Another way to be peaceful is to play Christian music in your home, car, or office. Music moves and motivates people, so turn on some praise music and let it minister to you. There is power in praise music. Worshipping our Lord has a soothing effect on us. It is a great way to relax, calm down, and enjoy peace. This is how we truly experience the peace of God.

This may sound strange but being organized helps with peacefulness as well. My wife is super organized and I love it. She has a dry-erase calendar on the wall that shows four months; with four kids this really helps us stay organized, which helps keep the peace. Having a budget is a form of organization as well. Giving every dollar a name will help you keep your sanity.

In summary, eliminating anything that annoys your spouse would bring much peace and tranquility to your marriage. All you have to do is ask them what annoys them and they will tell you. From leaving lights on to leaving your underwear on the floor, eliminating these bad habits will make things more peaceful around the homestead.

I urge, then, first of all, that petitions, prayers, intercession
and thanksgiving be made for all people - for kings
and all those in authority, that we may live peaceful
and quiet lives in all godliness and holiness.

1 Timothy 2:1–2

Chapter 24
BE CREATIVE

WE SERVE A very creative God. According to Fact Monster, there are about 950,000 species of insects, 9,956 species of birds, 30,000 species of fish, 8,240 species of reptiles, and 5,416 species of mammals on our planet.[15] Wow, that's a lot of species and I just named a few. What about the billions of stars and the fact that God has a name for every one of them according to Psalms 147:4? Since we are created in God's image, we are creative too.

Being creative involves doing things out of the ordinary. We all have morning routines of getting ready, getting the kids ready, eating breakfast, and getting to school and work. We also have routines when we come home from school or work. And then we have dinner routines, bedtime routines, Sunday routines, and vacation routines. To be creative, just think of ways to *not* be routine. Do something to break up the monotony of life.

Try something different for breakfast like make pancakes, omelets, or go out for breakfast. Making love is usually a great thing to do in the morning, assuming it's out of the ordinary. For lunch, meet your spouse at their workplace or go to a restaurant you have been wanting to try.

For dinner, make something together that you have never made before. Take a gander at the cookbook and decide what to try and just do it. Invite a couple *that you both like* over for dinner or have a picnic somewhere. Go to Smoothie King and have a big smoothie for dinner. Just think outside the box. I'm thinking Chinese now …

For bedtime, give each other a foot massage—set the timer for equal pleasure. Go buy new pajamas and wear them or don't wear anything at all! Stay up late and watch a movie. Swap sides of the bed, rearrange your bedroom, sleep somewhere else in the house, or read a book together.

For Sundays, serve together somewhere in the church. Take doughnuts and orange juice to a small group - your kids would love this for their class too. Go to lunch somewhere and pay for someone else's meal. Take a nap together. It's just healthy to get out of our routines for a change.

Marriage should not be boring; it should be enjoyed and exciting. So reflect on your marriage and pray and ask God to help you be creative. Life is too short to be bored to death. Put the effort in your marriage and start today.

In the beginning God created the heavens and the earth.

Genesis 1:1

Chapter 25
BE FLEXIBLE

WE MUST LEARN to be flexible in marriage due to the fact that men and women are so different. And sometimes God puts a man and woman together that don't have anything in common except their relationship with God. The following letter is from my good friend, Allan Taylor:

Linda and I are opposites. I'm the oldest sibling; she is the youngest. I am more serious; she is a party waiting for a place to happen. I am more introverted; she is more extroverted. I am thrifty; she enjoys spending. Therefore, when we got married there was a great potential for growth in our marriage, but there was also a great potential for divorce!

Like all couples our marriage has had challenges—financial struggles, raising three children, upgrading our small, inexpensive houses, three career changes, and three out-of-state moves. What held our marriage together? Our relationship with Christ!

Before we married, we had committed our lives and our marriage to God. Love for God and love for each other

will see you through! The Apostle Paul said, "And now abides faith, hope, and love, these three; but the greatest of these is love" (1 Corinthians 13:13). Love can withstand many things—struggles, trials, challenges, and yes, even abuse—but it cannot withstand neglect! So whatever you do, keep love alive!

Flexibility is an important key in marriage. You have to go with the flow and trust God in what comes your way. We have to respect each other's differences and see them as a positive thing and not a negative thing. If we were just alike it would be boring. God puts a twist on things to make it more interesting. Being different actually brings balance. But you can't have balance without flexibility.

I know what it is to be in need, and I know what it is to have plenty. I have learned the secret of being content in any and every situation, whether well fed or hungry, whether living in plenty or in want. I can do all this through Him who gives me strength.

Philippians 4:12–13

Photo by: Nathan Dumlao on Unsplash

Chapter 26
BE ATTRACTIVE

"EVERY GIRL'S CRAZY about a sharp-dressed man." When I hear that I think about ZZ Top and *Duck Dynasty*. Most men are "sight oriented," but I'm sure a woman likes to see her man dressed up from time to time. I realize it's impossible to be attractive all the time—especially in the mornings when we roll out of bed—but we should never give up looking good for our mate.

I'm not talking about dressing like Ward and June Cleaver from *Leave It to Beaver* (TV show from the '50s and '60s) every day. But I also don't think that we should wear sweats every day either. I know those black yoga pants are comfortable, but try to wear something different periodically. If your underwear has more than three holes in them then it's time to throw them away. I had to do this the other day and it grieved my soul.

Dr. Adrian Rogers said, "Even an old barn needs a coat of paint now and then." He was referring to women wearing makeup. I do not like a lot of makeup but it can magnify your beauty (I had to be careful how I said that). My wife just wears eye makeup, which enhances her beautiful brown eyes.

Men, we need to be attractive to our wives. We need to do our best to lose the gut (see chapter 28) and strengthen our bodies. Did you know that the more in shape you are the more respect you get? Most men want to be respected, so being in shape is one way to gain it. Also, men need to be well-groomed for their wives. We need to pluck that one 1-inch hair between our eyes, those nose hairs that are sticking out, and trim the ear hairs. We need to trim our finger- and toenails. I told a friend of mine the other day who had long fingernails, "Are you gonna cut those or paint them?" We also need to smell good. We just celebrated Father's Day and I asked for cologne so I could smell good. Kari bought a big bottle of it that cost $70! I reckon I need to use it because she wants me to smell good too.

Being attractive is more than how you dress, smell, and look. A person with a great attitude, personality, and sense of humor is very attractive to most. Someone who is physically fit can be attractive too. Someone with a compassionate heart is also attractive. So, put all those together and you can be one good-looking person! Which ones do you need to work on? Don't let yourself go—strive to be attractive to your spouse.

Once again, this is a communicative subject. All we have to do is ask our spouse, "What can I do to be more attractive?" Be sure to brace yourself and listen without firing back your defense. Remember, it's the small things that make a big difference.

She sets about her work vigorously;
her arms are strong for her tasks.

Proverbs 31:17

Photo by: Kay on Unsplash

Chapter 27
Be Accountable

When I was a student minister at Oakland Baptist Church in Corinth, MS, I started an accountability group with about five guys (not the burger joint). I had listened to an Andy Stanley sermon on accountability and realized I needed it. We met every Wednesday for lunch at The Dinner Bell and asked each other the following questions:

- Have you been in the Word daily?
- How is your prayer life and how can we pray for you?
- Are you tithing and spending His money wisely?
- Have you spent quality time with your family?
- Have you been exposed to sexually explicit material in any form?
- Has your speech been encouraging and not gossipy?
- Have you missed church?
- Are you above reproach in your relationships?
- Have you just lied about any of your previous responses?

More than 17 years later, I am still using the power of accountability with different guys. When you have to answer these questions every week in total honesty, it will help you be consistent in your walk with the Lord. Accountability is like a safety net to a tightrope walker. We all need someone asking us the hard questions and then encouraging us when we fall.

Husbands and wives should be accountable to each other spiritually, sexually, financially, and parentally. We should ask each other about our quiet times with the Lord and how that's going. We look out for each other if we notice someone flirting with our mate while the other may not notice it. I felt responsible for telling Kari how men think. She was shocked to say the least. We also help each other with the budget. Since Kari handles the money, she will tell me when I don't need to use the debit card because things are tight. We have each other's back on parenting as well and being on the same team when it comes to parental decision making.

However, each spouse should have an accountability partner, in addition to their spouse. This should be a godly person of the same gender who is trustworthy. Ask God to show you who this might be and go up and ask them. I recommend meeting once a week. This is different than having a *mentor* couple. This is about your personal spiritual growth. We do not stand before the throne of God after we die as a couple. Everyone has to stand before God alone.

Accountability is a big deal in life and in our walk with the Lord. As a matter of fact, right after I wrote this chapter, a church leader I know was arrested on patronizing prostitution and human trafficking. To my knowledge he was not in an accountability group asking the hard questions. Now, the state is holding him accountable behind bars. I trust he will repent and allow God to help him finish strong. Accountability is not 100% effective but it sure does help.

As iron sharpens iron, so one person sharpens another.

Proverbs 27:17

Photo by: Curtis MacNewton on Unsplash

Chapter 28

BE IN SHAPE

OKAY, THIS IS a touchy subject for some, and they may not even read this chapter. Before you go to the next chapter, please know that this has a *lot* to do with having a great marriage. The more in shape you are, the better your sex life will be. *That* ought to motivate you. If not, what about this: Regular exercise enhances arousal for women and decreases the chance of men having erectile dysfunction. Are you moody, have low self-esteem, have low energy, are not impressed with yourself in the mirror, or are getting sick often? Keep reading.

Being in shape makes you feel better about yourself and makes you more attractive for your spouse. Have you heard the expression "You are easy on the eyes"? When you feel better about yourself, you are more apt to wear sexy clothing for your spouse. You will have confidence in how you look. This keeps the spark alive. Regular exercise gives you the energy to even *want* to have sex.

If you are a novice at this, get advice from your doctor before you start. Also, seek counsel from a trainer of some sort and get on a workout plan. The more in shape you are the better employee, employer, dad, mom, husband, and wife you can be because you will have energy and stamina to do things. Working out can be fun to do together. You can set goals and help each other achieve them. This can be quality time together.

Exercise can even help you sleep better. Just don't do it right before bedtime, it may take you a long time to go to sleep because your heart rate is up. Exercise can help you live longer, enjoy your family longer, and serve the Lord longer to advance the Kingdom of God. Exercise prevents weight gain and gives your body a better shape. Exercise helps prevent so many diseases like cardiovascular disease, type-2 diabetes, depression, and certain types of cancer. It also helps improve your mood, which helps in any marriage. Who likes to be around a moody person?

I started lifting weights and exercising in high school and haven't stopped since. It *really does* affect my mood and attitude if I haven't worked out in 3 or 4 days. I feel terrible and become a little grouchy. I currently walk on the treadmill about every day for 20–45 minutes. I also use exercise bands and weights to do a full-body workout two-three times a week. I also swim as much as possible. There are many nights after dinner that our family will take a walk or ride bikes together as well.

Exercise should be a priority like eating. Speaking of eating, regular exercise makes you *want* to eat healthy. They go hand in hand. It wouldn't make sense to work out for an hour and then go eat a hamburger, fries, and milkshake. You would feel like you blew the workout, causing it to be null and void. I realize this happens sometimes and it's okay from time to time, but it shouldn't be the norm.

So start today. Don't wait until Monday (unless today is Monday). Make exercise a priority. Write down a plan and make it happen. Get your heart rate up and keep it up for at least 20 minutes a day. Then work every muscle group including your abs. There are so many workout plans. Start easy or light and progress from there. You will be glad you did and so will your spouse and kids. If you join a gym, be sure to go with your spouse and dress modestly. This ensures accountability and prevents being a stumbling block to others.

Do you not know that your bodies are temples of the Holy Spirit, who is in you, whom you have received from God? You are not your own; you were bought at a price. Therefore honor God with your bodies.

1 Corinthians 6:19–20

Chapter 29
BE TEACHABLE

DO YOU KNOW your spouse's love language? What about their spiritual giftedness? Do you know how your marriage is a picture of the Gospel? Are you a mentor to a younger couple or are you being mentored? Is your marriage a good model for marriage? Do people come to you for advice on marriage? Has anyone ever complimented your marriage? Have you taken a marriage class lately? Have you been to a marriage conference lately? Okay, enough questions. There are just so many ways to pour into your marriage.

Kari and I speak at marriage conferences and love to see couples of all ages attend. No matter how long you have been married, there is always room for improvement. Being teachable means you are willing to learn. Once again, have you learned to speak your spouse's love language? This is one of the most important things I've learned in marriage. I can't emphasize this enough.

The person you can learn from the most is your spouse. Just ask them how you can improve as their spouse and sit back and listen without getting hacked off. I also encourage you to discover each other's spiritual giftedness and take a personality test. I highly recommend that you know your spouse's love language, spiritual giftedness, and personality type. These will help you understand each other and help you get along.

Marriage is a picture of the Gospel and we need to represent it well. Paul tells us in Ephesians 5:30–31 (ESV), "*Therefore a man shall leave his father and mother and hold fast to his wife, and the two shall become one flesh. This mystery is profound, and I am saying that it refers to Christ and the church.*" The man leads, loves, and serves his wife because that is how Jesus gives Himself to His bride. And the wife respects, submits to, and helps her husband because that is how the Church of God follows Jesus.

Our marriages should be great role models for our children, family, friends, church, and the world. Let's be that example for Christ.

Hopefully, your church offers marriage and parenting classes. If not, ask your pastor about it. There are several marriage DVDs to watch to learn from, and it's really easy to push "play." If your church doesn't offer a marriage retreat, there are many to choose from around the nation. Never stop learning how to have a great marriage.

Whoever disregards discipline comes to poverty and shame, but whoever heeds correction is honored.

Proverbs 13:18

Photo by: Jonathan Borba on Unsplash

Chapter 30
BE INTENTIONAL

IN ORDER TO be intentional, we have to be intentional about our good intentions. We all have good intentions to some extent, but we must carry them out. Good intentions and procrastination are first cousins. For example, how long have you been meaning to fix that leaky faucet or a leaky roof? Days go by, even months, and then one day the leak becomes a flood. Many times we procrastinate so long that disaster hits. Then we kick ourselves, saying, "I should've fixed that leak a long time ago. I really *intended* on doing it."

This happens in marriages often. Couples get so busy with raising kids or climbing the ladder of success that they neglect their marriages. Sometimes 10 or 20 years go by and they have drifted very far apart. I know it's difficult, but you must make your marriage a priority. Many things hinge on you having a great marriage. Many couples had good intentions, but now so much water has gone under the bridge they end up in divorce. Many couples have grown so far apart that when the kids leave they do not know each other very well. A great marriage takes intentionality.

So, *man up* or *woman up* and talk about your issues or go see a Christian counselor. Take that class or go on that marriage retreat.

Get a marriage mentor who can point you in the right direction and give you sound advice. Write down your intentions, prioritize them, and do them. Your marriage is worth it. There is a lot at stake — mainly your children and the Gospel. If you jump out of this marriage based on irreconcilable differences, you might just have irreconcilable differences in the next marriage. So, go ahead and work through them in the first marriage so that you won't have all the baggage going into the second marriage. Be intentional now.

All you need to say is simply 'Yes' or 'No'; anything beyond this comes from the evil one.

Matthew 5:37

Chapter 31

BE PREPARED

IF YOU ARE reading this book as preparation for marriage, you are doing the right thing. So many couples plan for the wedding and not the marriage. Reading marriage books is one of the best things you can do prior to marriage. As I am writing this, I am about to conduct a premarital counseling session. In this session, I will ask them to share their salvation testimony. God tells us *not to be unequally yoked*, which means Christians should not marry non-Christians (2 Corinthians 6:14). Then we talk about beliefs, personalities, spiritual giftedness, and love languages. I then assign reading and challenge them not to copulate until the wedding night.

After the wedding we should prepare for many things. (By the way, life is about relationships and preparation.) We should prepare how we are going to spend, save, and give money. Many people just talk about spending and saving, but giving is where the fun begins. You never miss what you give away.

We should prepare for children. Having children is such a blessing, but it can also be stressful on your marriage. Many times a couple focuses on their children and neglects their marriage. The best thing you can do for your children is to love your spouse. It's wise to make sure the foundation of marriage is strong before you have children, if possible. Plan to continue to work on your marriage after children. Couples need to continue to have date nights and getaways without children.

Being prepared means you have to plan. Kari and I are both planners but we still have to work on it. Christmas, birthdays, Valentine's Day, and anniversaries come every year so plan on them. Couples must share their expectations on all of these in order for them to be happy occasions. Kari and I currently live 11 hours away from both of our parents. So every time we go home we have to discuss how we are going to spend our time. We have to equal out the time between the families. This takes planning. I was talking to a couple the other day and they had just had an anniversary. They were so busy that they'd failed to plan for it, and it ended up being just another day. No special meal, gifts, or getaway—sad. Even if you're broke, you can do something to celebrate.

Speaking of Christmas, how do you plan for the expense of it since it comes every year at the same time? Many families do not plan for it and put everything on credit cards and spend the next year paying them off with interest. This is a vicious cycle. The best thing to do is to plan on it by bank drafting a certain amount of money from your checking account every month into a Christmas savings account. When December rolls around, you have enough for Christmas. Just don't overspend. Don't forget to include travel costs and food along with the gifts. This helps Christmas not to be so stressful. It should be the most wonderful time of the year because Jesus came. He didn't have to come, you know, but He did!

Please know that Satan hates your marriage and he will do everything in his power to destroy it. You must be prepared for his attacks. He will always try to separate what is supposed to be one. One way he does this is through finances. He'll encourage you to have separate accounts. He'll try to separate you in space by luring one of you to take a job in another city for more money. Satan will also try to steal away your intimacy by reminding you of your past or by enticing you with another man or woman. We must guard against this by putting on the armor of God (Ephesians 6:11–18). We must take captive every thought unto the obedience of Christ (2 Corinthians 10:5). We must prepare ourselves with accountability and boundaries. When the devil comes knocking, let Jesus open the door. Let the Word of God be your defense. Jesus did.

Suppose one of you wants to build a tower. Won't you first sit down and estimate the cost to see if you have enough money to complete it? For if you lay the foundation and are not able to finish it, everyone who sees it will ridicule you, saying, 'This person began to build and wasn't able to finish.'

Luke 14:28–30

Chapter 32

BE FRUGAL

FINANCES ARE USUALLY the second top reason for divorce, so nip this in the bud before it can trouble your marriage. By the way, the number-one reason for divorce is lack of communication. The goal for every couple should be to be debt free. Being frugal doesn't mean you can't have any fun. It just means you are smarter and more patient. It's kind of like the phrase from Dave Ramsey, "If you *will* live like no one else, later *you can* live like no one else."[16]

Frugal means "prudently saving or sparing; not wasteful." Other words would include *thrifty, careful, prudent,* and *scrimping.*[17] I'm sure several people come to mind when you think of this word. My two sons and I went on a mission trip to Haiti years ago with our student ministry. We did door-to-door evangelism, played with children, led backyard Bible clubs, hard labor, etc. Many people in Haiti live day-to-day not knowing from where their next meal will come. Most of the people we interacted with did not have electricity, running water, or indoor plumbing in their huts. For their toilet, they would dig a deep hole in their backyard. It did not smell very good and we think we have it bad.

This trip to Haiti made us realize how wasteful we are in America.

We throw away so much food and water and live like kings and queens in luxury compared to most Haitians. We are so blessed to have access to clean water and an abundance of food. We need to learn to be more frugal and share more. I encourage you to fast through a meal or a day and see how it feels to be hungry, and of course to pray for those who do not have enough food or water.

Kari and I try to be frugal. We do not feel that we are pack rats. If we haven't used something within a year's time, we sell it, give it, junk it, or take it to the thrift store. We go through our closets a couple of times a year and take out all the clothes and shoes we haven't worn in a while and give them away to relatives, friends, or the thrift store. God is a God of order and not clutter. So don't build bigger barns to store your stuff or rent a storage building. Renting storage space should only be temporary. Be a blessing to others. We should all take inventory of our stuff and declutter and be generous.

There is a big difference between a *need* and a *want*. I highly recommend you read David Platt's book *Radical*. It will help you understand the difference between a *need* and a *want*. Kari is pretty frugal. She's pretty too. She buys half of her clothes at consignment stores. One man's junk is another man's treasure. Here is a list of ways to be frugal:

- Mow your own grass.
- Three things you need to know before buying a house: location, location, location. Check your surroundings, school system, etc.
- Buy vehicles that have good resale value. Even certain colors have better resale value.
- Each year, shop different auto, home, and health insurance companies.

- Use coupons.
- Be patient when shopping for cars, houses, vacation rentals, big purchases, etc.
- Be patient and see that awesome movie when it's available on TV.
- Plan your meals for the week.
- Eat at home more often.
- Share a meal at a restaurant.
- If you have a credit card, pay it off every month. Debit cards and cash produce more accountability.
- Check your bills to make sure they didn't add any expense without your approval. This happens often, unfortunately.
- Program your thermostat to work when needed.
- Make sure your house is well-insulated.
- Buy term life insurance.
- Use cash for almost everything.
- Buy a water bottle and refill it instead of buying bottled water all the time.
- Don't go grocery shopping while you are hungry.
- Get everything in writing when doing deals.
- Have a written budget and stick to it.
- Go on vacation at off-peak times.
- Always park in the shade or put a protective cover in the dash of your car to prevent the sun from causing your dash or leather to dry up and crack. Protect your investment!
- Quit expensive habits that are bad for you.
- Instead of buying brand-new things, buy used ones like exercise equipment.
- Look for a bank that has free checking.
- This may be gross for some, but use your towel to dry off

a couple of times before you wash it.

- Paint your own nails.
- Change your own oil and filter in your car.
- Get a friend or family member to cut your hair for a cheaper price.
- Increase your car and house insurance deductibles.
- Work out at home. This is what I do. But if you need the accountability then stay in the gym.
- Buy airline tickets in advance or shop for last-minute deals.
- Buy cars that do not require premium gas.
- Buy in bulk if you know you will use it.
- Learn to haggle or deal with people. Remember cash talks.
- Instead of hiring a job out, do it yourself. Just YouTube it.
- Buy quality. Mom used to say, "Good things are not cheap and cheap things are not good." I do this with clothing and shoes because I wear the heck out of them.
- Don't waste water. A friend of mine will fill up a bucket of water while waiting for the water to get hot before he takes a shower. He then pours the bucket of water into the toilet for flushing. Now that's frugal!
- If you have a garage, park your car in it to keep it out of the weather. Your car is probably your 2nd biggest expense.
- Turn off lights. If you're like me, I go around the house turning off lights ALL THE TIME.

The wise store up choice food and olive oil, but fools gulp theirs down.

Proverbs 21:20

Chapter 33

BE GENEROUS

GENEROSITY IS A beautiful thing. Everyone loves to be around a generous person. Being generous means going out of your way to be kind to your spouse. For example, when you get up from the table to fill your drink, ask your spouse do they need anything while you're up. Generosity leads to happiness. The more generous you are to your spouse, the happier they will be with you and hopefully it will be reciprocated.

Being generous means to give freely and abundantly. It is putting their needs above yours. When you are generous to your spouse it means you value them. The key is to know your spouse and what they like. When you know what they like, give it to them. Whether it is sex, a back rub, flowers, helping with the dishes, opening the car door, kissing them, quality time, hugging them, giving them compliments, gifts, or whatever.

Generosity ranks up there with sexual intimacy, commitment, and communication for marital success and satisfaction. It's the "open hands" principle. We should have open hands to receive and to give. We need to be a conduit for the Lord to give to us and *through* us. As a spouse, we should learn how to receive and give generosity.

Some people do not *receive* well. They don't know how to take a compliment or an act of service. They almost reject them. This can hurt the person's feelings trying to give.

We all need to be more generous with our time, money, talents, words, and things. It takes time to grow a marriage. So be careful about being so busy that you are like ships that pass in the night. Prioritize your time together. Be generous with your money. Remember, it's really not your money anyway. God owns everything. Invest in your mate. Make memories together. Don't procrastinate trips and experiences until you are retired. You may die before then or you may be too old to enjoy them. Save up for the trip or experience and enjoy them with each other.

Use your talents to fortify your marriage. Some people use their talents for everyone else except their spouse. I realize I'm being vague, but I am trusting the Holy Spirit to speak to you here. Be generous with your words. One husband said, "I told my wife I loved her at the wedding, why does she need to hear it again?" Use your words to remind your mate how much you love and care for them. Isn't it amazing how words can make or break you and your marriage? Oh, the power of the tongue. "Oh, be careful, little mouth, what you say." We really need to think before we speak.

When you get married, your things are not your things anymore. This may come as a shock to some of you, but when you marry it's not me, myself, and I—it's yours, mine, and ours. The two shall be one (Mark 10:8). What you have belongs to your spouse as well now. Like, if you have a boat that you only use two times a year, your wife might suggest that you sell it. You can't say, "This is my boat, I'm keeping it." You need to value your wife's opinion and realize it's hers too now. Selling it might be the right thing to do for the benefit of the marriage. You might need that money to invest in your marriage, such as a marriage retreat or conference or just a getaway.

A generous person will prosper; whoever refreshes others will be refreshed.

Proverbs 11:25

Chapter 34
BE VERBAL

COMMUNICATION IS EVERYTHING in marriage. We must communicate feelings, love, expectations, knowledge, experiences,
godliness, dreams, needs, wants, desires, longings, facts, encouragement, money matters, goals, etc. Many times, extroverts marry
introverts. Our marriage is an example. God has a sense of humor.
The extroverts wish the introverts talked more and the introverts
wish the extroverts would shut up. As in our marriage, you *will*
need to meet in the middle. The extrovert will learn to listen more,
and the introvert will learn to talk more.

Couples need to give each other undivided attention. This means
turning the TV and phone off and looking each other in the eyes.
Guys are usually not very good at this. If you will notice, when guys
are talking, they hardly ever look at each other in the eyes. Their
bodies are not face-to-face but tilted a little to the side as though
they are talking to someone else. This is so funny and true. So men,
you have to be intentional about this with your wife. Look her in the
eyes. And while you do, compliment how beautiful her eyes are.

Since men and women are so different, we need to ask clarifying
questions to verify what we heard. It is dangerous to assume the

motive behind what you hear from your spouse. So verify what they meant. It's ok to ask, "What did you mean when you said this?" This is just a wise thing to do to make sure you heard what they said. Also, most women want to talk it out and want you to listen to them. *They do not necessarily want a solution.*

Remember, you both are on the same team so support each other verbally. Don't just give advice. Instead, listen and encourage them along the way. Let them know you have their back. Many couples talk to each other as though they are on opposing teams. This is a great reminder. Teammates encourage, motivate, and build each other up. Rivals discourage, intimidate, and get puffed up at each other. Proverbs 15:1 says, "*A gentle answer turns away wrath, but a harsh word stirs up anger.*" So, when you *assume* your mate is trying to start an argument, respond with a gentle answer. We must think before we speak. Will what I say encourage or discourage? You are on the same team so don't work against each other.

My cousin, Whitney, said the best thing to do if you are about to get in an argument is to start taking off your clothes. I'll never forget that and I wish we would implement it! I double-dog dare you to try that and see how far the argument goes. Along those lines, it *is* a good idea to physically touch each other while communicating. I don't mean to touch in a sexual way but in a gingerly way. It is difficult to lash out at one another when you are tenderly touching each other.

The greatest advice on communicating touchy issues is to pray about them together. Allow the Spirit of God to help you deal with your controversy. Ask God to fill you with His Spirit and give you wisdom with the issue. God is for your marriage and He is here to help make it strong for your good and His glory. The Spirit will guide you unto all truth (John 16:13). So invite Him in and trust Him.

Without communication in marriage, spouses drift away. So, talk about everything. Be sure to have good timing on certain conversations. Please do not argue in front of your kids; it only breeds insecurity and fear in them. Go into the other room and shut the door to have your *discussion*—but with respect and gentleness. Once again, you are on the SAME TEAM. I said that with gentleness.

May these words of my mouth and this meditation of my heart be pleasing in your sight, LORD, my Rock and my Redeemer.

Psalms 19:14

Photo by: Shawn Fields on Unsplash

Chapter 35

BE TRANSPARENT

SINCE MARRIAGE IS the most intimate union in society, transparency must happen all the time. Intimacy means "into me you see," so in order to see inside we need to be transparent. It means being honest and sharing your feelings. Sharing their feelings is difficult for men in general but is essential in a marriage relationship.

For example, if you really want that new outfit, discuss it, and see if it fits in the budget. If you have a little cushion in the budget or a miscellaneous line item, use that for the outfit—even if you have to save up a few months to get it. It is not healthy to hide purchases or anything from your spouse.

If you feel like someone of the opposite sex is hitting on you, you need to tell your spouse. Kari warns me sometimes when she is sensing this. Let's be real: it feels good when someone is hitting on you because you are getting attention. However, this should be a major red flag for you and a warning to end it and let your spouse know.

We have to look out for each other by being open and clear. Transparency brings everything to light. This way, the devil will find it hard to get a foothold in your life. He loves doing things in secret and in the dark. That's why he is like a thief or a lion. They try to stay in the shadows and sneak up on their prey and steal and kill. Bring everything to the light and dispel the darkness (Ephesians 5:13).

Couples should not have to hide anything or be afraid of sharing anything with their mate. Transparency will strengthen your relationship. Remember, you are a team. We need to fight temptation together. Together, we are stronger. God made us different to make us one. We can't get stronger if we hide our weaknesses and differences from each other.

We led a marriage retreat in Gatlinburg, TN, and the theme was "Get Your Love Tank Full." One of the nuggets to implement in your marriage was to occasionally ask your spouse, "Is your love tank full?" Many times you don't want to ask that because you are afraid of their answer. This is true transparency to the core. Here's a good way to say it to your spouse: "Hey honey, I really want to please you, so will you tell me if and when your love tank isn't full because I want to keep it full?" Have a good attitude with it and say, "Hey, I'm coming to the Love Tank Station, I need a fill-up."

Nothing in all creation is hidden from God's sight.
Everything is uncovered and laid bare before the
eyes of Him to whom we must give account.

Hebrews 4:13

Chapter 36
BE KIND

HAVE YOU EVER heard the expression "Kill them with kindness?" If your spouse is being a jerk, bite your tongue and be kind to them. This takes a lot of willpower and you can't allow sarcasm in your kindness. Try it and watch the power of kindness and how it works on the jerk.

There are many ways to be kind to your spouse but I'll mention a few. One way is to praise them in public. It always helps if your spouse hears you praise them. This is a great way to encourage your spouse and motivate your marriage. It's always good to praise your spouse to your parents and their parents. Many spouses take jabs at their spouses in front of family members and it's just not healthy.

Another way to be kind is to show interest in their hobbies or friends. Hobbies and friends can sometimes pull couples apart, so it's wise to participate in their hobbies and get to know their friends. This is a great way to get to know your spouse and see how they act in their hobby and with their friends. This also establishes accountability in your marriage. It's always good to care about what your spouse cares about. There is a fine line here so be sure to give them their space.

Being kind means saying nice things to your spouse like "You look great in that outfit" or "I'm so proud of you." It's amazing how our words can soothe and satisfy someone. Being kind means doing things for your spouse. There is a plethora of kind things to do for your spouse. You could wash their car, put gas in their car, clean the house, fix whatever is wrong with the house, cook their favorite meal, plan a date night in every detail, or give them unexpected sex.

Another way to be kind is to not get so angry so easily. Control your temper. Calm down. Take a chill pill. Be calm, cool, and collected. Never raise your voice at your spouse. Don't be so negative. Look on the bright side of things. Don't take life so seriously and laugh a little. So, have a good attitude and *enjoy* marriage; don't just *endure* it.

Kindness benefits everyone. It brings joy to the giver, and peace to the receiver. Kindness is many times contagious. Being kind to your spouse many times will be reciprocated. However, many times we have this attitude of, "If you will, then I will." We should say, "I will, even if you won't."

*A kindhearted woman gains honor, but ruthless
men gain only wealth. Those who are kind benefit
themselves, but the cruel bring ruin on themselves.*

Proverbs 11:16–17

Chapter 37
BE A SERVANT

JESUS CAME TO serve and not to be served, and we are supposed to imitate Him. I know what you're thinking: *But I'm not Jesus.* However, if you have the Spirit of God in you (and if you are a Christian, you do), then the same Spirit that served through Jesus can serve through **you**. So, every day we should pray that the Spirit of God will serve our spouses through us. God will even help you do this with gladness and a smile.

Okay, this just happened yesterday: Kari spilled some of my French Vanilla Creamer on the floor and wiped it up with a dry rag. Well, it dried and there was still a smudge on the wood floor from the creamer because she didn't use a wet rag to clean it. At first, I thought, *she made this mess and she will notice it later and clean it*. Instead, I decided to serve her. I sprayed it and wiped it clean. By the way, I didn't even do it in front of her. She may not know until she reads this book. She *better* read this book! JK

Chick-fil-A has a great saying. Every time I say, "Thank you" to one of their workers they say, "My pleasure." It really should be "our pleasure" to serve our spouse. Not everyone *gets* to be married and have a significant other. We have the *opportunity* to serve our spouses. We should try to out-serve each other. Let's do things for our spouses before they have to ask.

Here are some ways to serve each other:

- Leave the toilet seat down for her.
- Prepare dinner when she is working late.
- Run their bathwater for them.
- Write a love note each day for a month or maybe on their birthday month.
- Wash the dishes for a whole day, month, year, or to infinity and beyond.
- Bring them breakfast in bed (if they like to eat breakfast).
- Take them on a surprise getaway.
- Fulfill something on their bucket list.
- Warm their car for them on a cold morning.
- Let your wife drive the newer and more dependable vehicle.
- Instead of doing your hobby, spend time with your spouse.
- Do the laundry and put it away. (Be sure you know where everything goes.)
- Pay someone to clean the house.
- Do a chore for your spouse that you know they hate to do.
- Take the kids to school for a week, month, or year.
- Clean the toilets inside and out.
- Clean the blinds.
- Clean the baseboards.
- Clean your ears and stop saying, "Huh?"
- Do the grocery shopping (unless your spouse loves to do it).

- Iron or take their clothes to the cleaner. (Better ask first on this one.)
- Give your mate a gift card to their favorite store.
- Bathe and get all the kids in bed and let your spouse watch a movie or take a long bath.

Each of you should use whatever gift you have received to serve others, as faithful stewards of God's grace in its various forms.

1 Peter 4:10

Photo by: Christina Wocintechchat on Unsplash

Chapter 38
BE A MENTOR

BEING A MENTOR means to assist, help, encourage, teach, counsel, sponsor, or support someone. Everyone needs a mentor even though pride gets in the way and says, "I can handle it on my own." We all need someone to seek advice from on many different levels. Why not *be* that someone? I know we've already touched on this but there is a huge shortage of marriage mentors. Allow God to use the wisdom He's given you to help someone else. I realize you do not know it all but go ahead and teach what you know. If you wait until you know it all, you'll never teach anyone anything because you'll never know it all.

The first thing to do to become a mentor is to focus on *your* marriage and make sure *you* are becoming the husband and wife that God has called you to be and implementing the things in this book.

The second thing is to pray that God will connect you with someone to mentor. You can't just say to someone, "Hey, can I mentor you in your marriage?" Allow God to connect you and speak through you.

The third possible thing to do would be to teach or facilitate a marriage class at church or somewhere else. There are many great marriage studies in media to just push "play" and lead in discussion. Tap into the wisdom that is already out there.

A fourth way is to read a marriage book together with a class and discuss it each week. Every church should teach on marriage, parenting, and finances every year. I challenge you to be a mentor and allow God to use you to help marriages across the land.

If you are going to be a mentor, be a biblical mentor. Make sure you understand God's perspective on marriage and divorce. He is *for* marriage and He *hates* divorce. He created marriage with Adam and Eve and it is still His plan between men and women. Marriage is that great union and bond between a man and a woman where the two fall in love and become one and become the foundation of a healthy family. This is the order of Almighty God and He *does* know it all.

God tells us there are two clear grounds for divorce: (1) sexual immorality (Matthew 5:32; 19:9) and (2) abandonment by an unbeliever (1 Corinthians 7:15). Confession, forgiveness, reconciliation, and restoration are always the first steps and the ultimate goal. Divorce should only be viewed as a last resort from these two issues. Remember *"with God all things are possible"* (Mark 10:27).

Couples need encouragement and practical solutions to their marital problems. Let's allow the Lord to do that through us. Let's be an ambassador for Him. Let's open our mouths and motivate marriages. Let's be countercultural and speak good about marriage instead of taking shots at it and downplaying it. Who can you encourage today?

*And the things you have heard me say in the
presence of many witnesses entrust to reliable people
who will also be qualified to teach others.*

2 Timothy 2:2

Chapter 39

BE SPIRIT-LED

BEING LED BY the Spirit of God is a constant filling. Every day, we should ask the Spirit to fill us to overflowing. Once you accept what Jesus did for you on the cross and receive Him into your heart, God places His Spirit inside you—never to leave you. However, we sometimes quench the Spirit. You see, we as Christians have the Spirit of God in us, but we also still have the sinful nature. The one that you feed the most is the one who will win. So feed the Spirit and be led by the Spirit.

This is by far the secret to living the victorious, abundant life in Christ. Many times people get saved and then try to live on their own instead of by the Spirit. God's Spirit wants to have dominion in your life. Life can be fun and exciting with the Spirit in control. The Spirit will help you do God's will for your life. The Spirit will help you understand God's Word—the Bible. Jesus tells us, *"But when He, the Spirit of truth, comes, He will guide you into all the truth. He will not speak on His own; He will speak only what He hears, and He will tell you what is yet to come"* (John 16:13). Just about every time before I have my quiet time, I ask the Spirit to guide me and teach me.

The Spirit will help you be a better husband or wife. He will help you make wise decisions. He will help you guard your tongue. He will give you creative ideas to enhance your marriage. We have to walk in the Spirit, wait on the Spirit, and rest in the Spirit. The Holy Spirit will help mold you into the image of Jesus—which is the goal of every believer (Romans 8:29).

I love this verse that tells us that God, Jesus, and the Holy Spirit are on our side: *"May the grace of the Lord Jesus Christ, and the love of God, and the fellowship of the Holy Spirit be with you all"* (2 Corinthians 13:14). Let that encourage you today. Let it wash over you like a warm shower. Embrace the Holy Trinity and all that He has and is for you. He loves you with an everlasting love. He loves you unconditionally and wants the best for you—His best. So let the Spirit lead you into His will and image. He has great plans for you (Jeremiah 29:11).

But the Helper, the Holy Spirit, whom the Father will send in My name, He will teach you all things, and bring to your remembrance all things that I said to you.

John 14:26

Photo by: Joe Hepburn on Unsplash

Chapter 40
BE PURPOSEFUL

HAVE YOU EVER thought, "What is the purpose of my marriage?" It's a great question we should all ask. Knowing the purpose will help us persevere. Knowing the purpose will help our attitudes. Knowing the purpose will help us understand our differences. In an article in *Christianity Today*, Ed Stetzer wrote this:

> **Erwin Lutzer correctly stated: "In marriage, the goal is holiness, not happiness." Marriage was intended to be a God-ordained commitment between one husband and one wife for one lifetime as one flesh. Sin has broken that, and we see those effects all around us. However, we have the Power in us to overcome. Christ is faithful to hold marriages together when they are centered on Him and His redemptive work on the cross. If our marriage is focused on holiness, happiness will inevitably follow. I've never met a couple who divorced because they were pursuing God too much.[18]**

Many times couples come into marriage as two selfish people. I was 29 years old before I married Kari, so I had 29 years of pleasing ... me. Now, I have a wife who is the opposite of me in every way and sees firsthand my shortcomings—and I see hers. Don't miss this! God gives us our spouse to help sharpen us and mold us into His image by pointing out things that are not right, such as anger, jealousy, hate, moodiness, weakness, selfishness, arrogance, pride, bitterness, insecurity, a critical spirit, gossip, foul language, worldliness, etc.

No one likes to be rebuked or criticized. However, we must humbly receive constructive criticism in order to grow and be sharpened. Your spouse will recognize weaknesses and even sin in your life that you never saw or felt. God often uses your spouse as a voice box to help make you holy and blameless. The more holy we are, the stronger our marriage will be for us and for God.

It is also important *how* we point these things out to our spouses. We must do it in a loving way and with the right tone. This can be done without nagging or a holier-than-thou attitude. Just pray about it and let the Spirit speak through you. So, if the Spirit prompts you to rebuke your spouse in love, do it with a gentle and loving spirit. After that, pray that the Holy Spirit will convict and restore your spouse and watch Him work.

I realize there are other purposes in marriage like fruitfulness, protection, provision, companionship, enjoyment, and oneness, but the main purpose is holiness. So continue to allow God to shape your marriage to reflect Christ and His church and to advance the kingdom of God. When we do marriage His way, we can love and be loved like we have always dreamed.

And we know that in all things God works for the good of those who love Him, who have been called according to His purpose.

Romans 8:28

BIBLIOGRAPHY

1   Feldhahn, Shaunti. *The Good News About Marriage: Debunking Discouraging Myths About Marriage and Divorce*. Colorado Springs: Multnomah Books, 2014.

2   Feldhahn, Shaunti. *The Good News About Marriage: Debunking Discouraging Myths About Marriage and Divorce*. Colorado Springs: Multnomah Books, 2014.

3   Chambers, Oswald. *My Utmost for His Highest*. Grand Rapids: Discovery House, 1992.

4   Rainer, Thom. *I Am a Church Member*. Nashville: B&H, 2013.

5   Berger, Lonnie. *Every Man a Warrior: Helping Men Succeed in Life*. Colorado Springs: NavPress, 2011.

6   Feldhahn, Shaunti. *The Good News About Marriage: Debunking Discouraging Myths About Marriage and Divorce*. Colorado Springs: Multnomah Books, 2014.

7   Chambers, Oswald. *My Utmost for His Highest*. Grand Rapids: Discovery House, 1992.

8   Chapman, Gary. *The 5 Love Languages: The Secret to Love That Lasts*. Chicago: Northfield, 2015.

9   Cloud, Henry, and John Townsend. *Rescue Your Love Life: Changing Those Dumb Attitudes & Behaviors That Will Sink Your Marriage.* Brentwood: Integrity, 2005.

10 Meyer, Joyce. *Do Yourself a Favor...Forgive: Learn How to Take Control of Your Life Through Forgiveness.* New York: FaithWords Hachette Book Group, 2012.

11 McGraw, Phillip. *Relationship Rescue: A Seven-Step Strategy for Reconnecting with Your Partner.* New York: Hyperion, 2000.

12 Chambers, Oswald. *My Utmost for His Highest.* Grand Rapids: Discovery House, 1992.

13 romance (n.d.). *The American Heritage® New Dictionary of Cultural Literacy, Third Edition.* Retrieved June 23, 2016 from Dictionary.com. Website: http://www.dictionary.com/browse/romance.

14 Cunningham, Ted. *Fun Loving You: Enjoying Your Marriage in the Midst of the Grind.* Colorado Springs: David C. Cook, 2013.

15 http://factmonster.com/ipka/.html. Fact Monster. © 2000–2013 Sandbox Networks, Inc., publishing as Fact Monster. 23 June 2016. http://www.factmonster.com/ipka/A0934288.html.

16 Ramsey, Dave. *The Total Money Makeover: A Proven Plan for Financial Fitness.* Nashville: Nelson, 2003.

17 "frugal." *Online Etymology Dictionary.* Douglas Harper, Historian. 23 June 2016. Dictionary.com. http://www.dictionary.com/browse/frugal.

18 http://www.christianitytoday.com/edstetzer/2012/september/pastors-that-divorce-rate-stat-you-quoted-was-probably.html. *Christianity Today*, September, 27, 2012.

CPSIA information can be obtained
at www.ICGtesting.com
Printed in the USA
FSHW021918030621
81985FS